Vanquishing Venture

Poems about freedom from drug and alcohol abuse, love
of nature, patriotism, the virus, travels, evangelism,
and finding hope and reconciliation with God.

TIM NEE

WESTBOW
PRESS®
A DIVISION OF THOMAS NELSON
& ZONDERVAN

WestBow Press books may be ordered through booksellers or by contacting:

WestBow Press
A Division of Thomas Nelson & Zondervan
1663 Liberty Drive
Bloomington, IN 47403
www.westbowpress.com
844-714-3454

ISBN: 978-1-6642-5721-4 (sc)
ISBN: 978-1-6642-5720-7 (hc)
ISBN: 978-1-6642-5722-1 (e)

Library of Congress Control Number: 2022902335

Print information available on the last page.

WestBow Press rev. date: 02/15/2022

CONTENTS

DEDICATION

I dedicate this collection of poems to all those on life's journey, from cradle to gurney. I hope you will enjoy this collection. Herein is a journey from the beaches of Florida to a stream in the wilderness of New Mexico. From the Mayan pyramids of Mexico and Central America to the big city hustle and bustle. Floating down the grand canal of Venice, to the mountains of garbage and ash heaps outside Mexico City. From India to the Northeast coast of the United States of America. Enjoying moments in nature and sharing the use and abuse of booze and drugs and finding sobriety because of the power of the Most High, through the gospel of Jesus Christ. From frowns to smiles, I hope there is something you can relate to for a while.

So, journey with me on my pen to paper moments I share. Experience a Spirit of hope and not a spirit of fear. Let your emotions go, it's okay to shed a tear, or maybe bring a smile for a while as you ponder what life is truly about and for what to eternally care. From the night aglow on the first Christmas day, to the One who overcame death and walked out of His grave. A poem inspired by a true story of one young woman held captive as a sex slave with all hope of freedom seemingly lost. To a tour of London, by the Queens palace to her Jewels, priceless the cost. To the streets and sights of Israel, to the Gethsemane Garden, where the burden of sin caused blood to be shed from the sweat of the Savior, at the excruciating pain of choosing to drink the cup to solve man's fallen condition.

You're invited to expand your horizons and to ponder with wonder from life's experiences shared here, from pits of hopeless despair to vast heights of glory, now there's a great story. From the experience of living through a world pandemic, to a beautiful sunset on the beach. So, enjoy the poems enclosed, be blessed, and realize you are not alone. No one knows from where the wind blows, may it blow here as we roam through the pages enclosed in this book that you hold. Venture ahead, be wise and be bold.

Peace to you, Tim Nee

INTRODUCTION

As men of old once donned a suit of armor as they ventured through life. We today, whether we know it or not, are in a spiritual battle. In the letter of Ephesians chapter six of the Bible. Christians are encouraged to stand firm and be suited up in the whole armor of God. Why? You may ask. In this present world with much chaos, sexual confusion, suicides even in our teen population, drug and alcohol addictions, uncertain future with a rampant virus. There are still dark principalities and powers at work to destroy us now, as when that letter to the church of Ephesus was penned by the apostle Paul centuries ago.

We can learn to live a life of victory and triumph because of Jesus, the Savior who was sent into this world to find and to save those who are lost, and He set out to destroy the work of our spiritual enemy, satan. When Jesus accomplished what He came for on earth and returned to heaven after His brutal sacrificial death, burial and resurrection. He said He would send us a Helper, and that Helper is the Holy Spirit. As we live out our lives, the dash between the dates of our birth and our death. May we come to learn that we are so loved by God. God is so kind and merciful and He longs to be gracious. He loves to restore anyone that has a soul in need of restoration and healing. God has seen all human history, and longs for a reconciled relationship with each of us.

He wants to set people free and to grant repentance, and bring healing, restoration and comfort to each person, but He will never override anyone's free will of whether a person chooses redemption provided or rejects God's provision of salvation and reconciliation with God.

There is power available to us that is like dynamite, to live a life which is a triumphant adventure, or vanquishing venture. The same power that raised Jesus from the dead is available to us. As we humble ourselves before the King of all kings, Jesus the Messiah. May we come to believe there is hope and that salvation is possible, and we can learn to know God personally. In a childlike faith and trust, instead of a religious practice, we can actually come to know God personally, which is eternal life.

We can suit up in our spiritual armor mentioned in Ephesians chapter 6 of the bible, which includes the helmet of salvation upon our head, the shield of faith to protect us from the devils' strategies, and we can learn to wield the sword of the spirit, God's word. So, suit up people, because we have an adversary that seeks human destruction. I choose with my free will to put my faith in the Lord of lords, and I hope you receive encouragement to do the same in this book.

Victory is ours only because of Jesus' victory when He rose from the dead in triumph that first resurrection morning, three days after His brutal crucifixion. Whatever anyone may be going through, realize the battle is not against flesh and blood, but is spiritual, and that battle is the Lords, and Jesus won already, and wants to share His victory with us. It is good to get to know the One who overcame death, because we will all breathe our last breath someday.

Our bodies are temples of God's Holy Spirit. He does not dwell in our temple automatically. When we enact our free will and invite Him into our lives, He comes to help us through this mortal life on earth. The Lord stands at the door of our heart and wants to come in, but He is a gentle man and would never override your free will. Will you choose to let Him in?

As the shepherds tended their sheep in a field outside Bethlehem over 2,000 years ago, they were visited by a host of angels. They were told not to be afraid, and that a Savior had been born. They were encouraged with words of peace and good will from God toward man. I pray that peace, which is available to whosoever chooses, will come to be known by you. To enact your free will, to believe, and venture through life walking in the light as a friend of God.

Possibly the last miracle Jesus did during His earthly life took place during His arrest in the Garden of Gethsemane in Jerusalem. Trying to defend Jesus, Peter unsheathed a sword, and wielded it and cut off the ear of one of the men among the arresting party, named Malchus. "But Jesus answered and said, "Permit even this." And He touched his ear and healed him."[1] There is significance in this story, as I read it one time, I felt I was supposed to read it again. Faith comes by hearing, and during possibly His last miracle, Jesus put a man's ear back on his head. Jesus wants people to hear and listen to the gospel, which causes our faith to grow; He healed an ear of not just any man, but a man named Malchus. The name Malchus means, my King. The Holy Spirit put the story together for me and revealed, that God wants people to hear the good news, and to get faith. When someone has faith, they come to believe and will exclaim, "my King" and

---

[1] Luke 22:51

make Jesus the King and Lord of their lives. Put Jesus on the throne of your life, and you will experience the peace and good will proclaimed by that heavenly host of angels 2,000 years ago in the skies over Bethlehem.

I hope and pray you will be encouraged through this first book that I have written, which reflects truth, and knowledge of the truth. In a world filled with lies, knowledge of truth brings freedom. Follow Jesus who once said, "I am the way and the truth and the life. No one comes to the Father except through Me."[2]

Be blessed!!!

---

[2] John 14:6

There is Hope

Some people don't know how to cope, I see
them with their head hanging low.

Downcast and in despair, some listen to the
suggestions of fear, and life just doesn't flow.

Some are angry, and just don't care,

Some just have a faraway stare.

Some go to the doctor, and he gives them a pill,

It makes coping easier for life's battles uphill.

Some have learned to set a new course,

Some have learned to go to life's source.

Some check out early, they can't keep pace.

They choose to leave life early and say goodbye to the human race.

Some, that's just not the case,

They make a lot of money and have a nice place.

Some buy whatever they want,

Some show off and like to flaunt.

Some are poor and live a life without the pocket to go to the store.

Some have nowhere to sleep so they rest on the floor.

Some choose to drink, but that doesn't make it better,

Some so lonely, don't even have someone
for which to write to a letter.

Some come to know the One who does care,

Some discover the possibility to draw near.

Some trudge along with all of life's woes,

They carry life's burdens from their head to their toes.

Their faces do not shine, they are sad and depressed.

Some laugh it off, as if there was not a care.

Some smoke a little something to take a stab at some peace.

Some spiral down, and don't see what's real.

Some learn to live in their alternative reality of
opinions they've formed, and think all is okay,

Without any regard of what God might say.

Some need to have their broken hearts heal,

If we go to the Source, He will not fail.

There is One that has overcome even death and
to the brokenhearted He is so near.

Some choose to reject Him, and about God they don't care.

Some choose religion or some spiritual force,
all kinds of intellectual thoughts,

In pride, they refuse to be humble and bow
to the One who's the source.

The One who can cleanse you and get you free from sin,

The One who can heal and restore and give us peace within.

There's a free gift, offered to all men, it is a gift of love,

sent from heaven above.

A gift you can't earn with all religious zeal,

One for which you can't beg, borrow or steal.

Some choose to have hope as an anchor for their soul,

Some choose to have a stocking full of coal.

I thank God for the One who gave His life for us all.

He paid the price for redemption from the fall.

We find life at the foot of the cross,

When one humbles themself and makes Jesus their Boss.

He's the King of all kings, and Lord of lords,

He's the Hope eternal when we cut life's cords.

So don't come to me with your guns or your swords,

I can't deny Him, my hope runs deep to the depths of my soul.

To know God more, is now my life goal,

Thankful for hope eternal in Jesus, the anchor of my soul.

The Wave

The never-ending momentum,

Some days all seems calm.

There's a stirring in the vastness,

At a touch all spins into motion.

His love is an ocean.

It's coming your way,

It's building up force.... swelling with mercy, grace, love and peace.

It's cresting, about to crash,

When suddenly in a moment of time,

The wave freezes silently still.

With your thoughts you could kill,

The wave stood still.

What a hard pill.

Existence without the refreshing, crashing waves of His love.

Your unbelief,

Your sin,

Your selfishness,

You're to be pitied.

You've allowed yourself to be ripped off.... But wait!!!!

I see you respond.

Those acts of Gods kindness have touched you deep within,

The vastness within.

Love and kindness could melt the entire sea,

But frozen in time are the waves that were meant for me.

I turn from all that would freeze the motion,

For He knows how to stir up the ocean.

LET the waves of mercy, grace, and love flow

Never again to be frozen in time.

Let's jump right in, the water is fine...
and learn to surf all in His time.

I yield myself to all You have planned, and I'm so grateful
to be refreshed on the shores of Your love.

Your waves are amazing,

Your grace is refreshment,

Your love is so deep, stir it up, set your ocean in motion.

Melt those who are frozen in time with Your kindness.

"Come now Let us reason together says the Lord, though your sins are like scarlet, they shall be as white as snow...." Isaiah 1:18

Flat Tire

My mind's eye sees a flat tire,

Reminded when life was trapped in a pit of muck and mire.

Some weary travelers' roads left us tattered, forlorn and torn,

Tire tread looks mighty worn.

Some rolled over something sharp and started to leak,

Some not elated, feeling exceedingly deflated.

I've come to know Someone that can pump us up,

He'll even invite us to sup, and drink from His cup.

Stuck on the side of life's road tried; trying ourselves to fix,

As the world rushes by with a glance, as we're stalled from the mix.

We've kicked our lug nuts all over the place.

Our lives, like Humpty's, broken pieces galore,

I know someone who loves to heal and restore.

Life would be great, with a new countenance on my face.

Sick of the pit of the muck and the mire?

Let's go to the One that can put new treads on our tire.

'Ready to let the rubber meet the road?

Are you heading towards the direction of the heavenly abode?

Tough time getting in gear?

Some are crippled with a spirit of fear.

Don't sit wounded on the side,

We need to learn, in Him to abide.

No longer stuck in my pain to hide,

We go to the One with a spear wound on His side.

In Him, on the wings of the wind, we're invited to glide.

"But those who wait on the Lord shall renew their strength; They shall mount up with wings like eagles, they shall run and not be weary, they shall walk and not faint." Isaiah 40:31

Help God

I have seen the purple mountain majesty.

I have stood for the song by Francis Scott Key.

I love this sweet land of liberty,

The pilgrims came to this land to be free from tyranny.

Seeking freedom to worship God without scorn.

There were triumphs and trials,

Sadness and smiles.

There were trails of tears, and birth pangs of this nation born,

There were battle lines drawn, a nation in two to be torn.

The smoke cleared, after many lives lost in our civil war.

To free the slaves was Lincolns great chore,

Not the end of the nation's strife, but we've
come a long way, believe that to the core.

God shed His grace on us,

If everyone walked with Jesus, it would be a plus.

Some hold on to hurts and pains from the past,

Some hate the flag that is raised on the mast.

Some focus on the color of skin,

When the real problem is sin.

I've driven through the fruited plains,

This country has so much good, but also many sin stains.

Some have done injustices which divide us all.

I say, "look to God, for He is not small."

God is great,

Turn to Him and reconcile before it's too late.

God said, "If my people who are called by My
name will humble themselves and pray,

And seek My face, and turn from their wicked ways,

Then I will hear from heaven and will forgive
their sin and heal their land."[3]

It's time to unite, but some are full of spite.

To take steps forward, we must learn to forgive the past,

That's if you want this country to last.

There are powers that be, that want to take over.

I don't believe in luck, or the four-leaf clover.

We need Gods help and we need it now,

---

[3] 2 Chronicles 7:14

Time for people to stop having a cow.

We can step forward, from darkness to light,

Set our sins at the cross, and seek Gods help, out of this plight.

Satan has tried to divide our house, so that it won't stand,

This is our country, We the Peoples land.

For those that seek to divide us, they can go pound sand.

Got to look at who's teaching what's taught,

This countries kids seem to hate us a lot.

There's hope for us all, days ahead bright as the sun,

We must repent and turn and see what God can get done.

There's no hope to go the godless route.

Let's build on the Rock....... Can we talk???

Indivisible, a house united, which does stand,

Let's communicate, talk things out, without mob rule demand.

Let's not be divided, like a house built on sinking sand.

We have a foundation of liberty for every American woman and man.

God created us all equal, lets live it out, YES we can!!!

May darkness be exposed, rotten to the core,

Let freedom ring, I implore.

God, please shed your grace on us, we need it today.

Let's progress, not go the hard route, like endless
days looking for a needle in the hay.

Forgive your neighbor, let us all pray.

So, let's raise old glory, not let present day
news be the end of our story.

We live in the greatest country in the history of man,

Let's learn to live in it according to God's plan.

The hour is getting late,

Let's stop all the hate.

We all have a short life, a moment in time,

Let's make it good, is that too sublime?

Let's live at peace with God and each other.

All heritage backgrounds let's treat as a brother.

United we stand, divided we fall,

Let's all hear God's voice and heed the call.

We live in a land that has had many a hero,

Let their lives count, and not live our lives as a zero.

Let's all pull together, and let God heal our land,

Stop forcing on all, what you demand.

Is it too much to ask to let FREEDOM ring?

Let's all bow our knees and humble ourselves
before the King of all kings.

Thank You

Thank You Your Royal Highness,

For Your love and kindness.

You dwell high above,

Holy Spirit, will You descend on us like a dove?

We will never comprehend the vastness of Your love.

Thank You, for restoring my soul,

Thank You, for redemption and making me whole.

Thanks for adopting me into the family, and making me your son,

Thank You, for the battles and victories won.

Thanks for freeing me from darkness bondage,
and up into Your marvelous light,

Thank You God for Your power and might.

Thanks, You've not given us a spirit of fear, nothing to cause fright.

Thank You, for faith that gives me strength,

Thanks, that to find the lost You go to any length.

Thanks for Your redemptive bloods power,
which washes white as snow,

Thanks for new garments with resurrection glow.

Thanks for the river from the threshold of
heaven, which deeply does flow,

Thank You Holy Spirit, our Helper, whose wind does blow.

Thanks that we can re-focus our mind on You
God, and You keep us in perfect peace.

Thank You, for hope in Christ as our soul's anchor;
the torment and choppy waves shall cease.

Thanks for keeping us from shipwreck and
learning to live with all hands-on deck.

To be sober and fruitful with You in life's walk,

To bless those who oppose, they grit their teeth and do mock,

Thank You Good Shepherd, that I'm part of your flock.

In this short life, I want to get to know You more,

I will thank You till my last breath is taken, and we
meet on the river of life's distant shore.

Thank You Lord for the invite.

And the Spirit and the bride say, "Come!" And let him who hears
say, "Come!" "And let him who thirsts come" "Whoever desires, let
him take the water of life freely." Revelation 22:17

Night Aglow

On that Christmas night, so long ago,

The sky lit up, it was all aglow.

The angels appeared in glory from on high,

To lowly shepherds who had never seen an angel fly.

They sang, "Glory to God, and on earth,
peace and goodwill toward man."

This was the birth of Gods master plan.

To reconcile sinful man, with a Holy God,

A Holy Savior was born, at this we APPLAUD.

The star shines bright, in the night sky above,

God's Son is born as an expression of God's love.

God with us, Emmanuel,

Because of His act of love, no longer on
the highway to destruction.

Jesus was born, to die on that tree,

By His sacrifice we can be totally set free.

I'm thankful, for the Lamb of God, first Christmas gift from above,

We will never find greater love.

My gift to God, in Him I put my TRUST,

His love will never fade, burn or rust.

To be a citizen of His kingdom,

Repent, make Him your Savior and Lord is a must.

The angels came that night to spread love and good cheer,

The shepherds were told, "have no fear."

Lift up the name of Jesus this day,

That baby was born and laid in the hay.

He grew to be Messiah, Savior and Lord,

To live without Him, no one can afford.

Thanks God, for your kindness and eternal love.

May your loving presence fill me like a Gentle Dove,

He came to heal sin and sorrow, heartache and pain,

With the blessed Savior, no sin leaves a stain.

I humbly kneel before the Prince of Peace,

My soul in His care, His love never to cease.

If you don't know Jesus, seek Him I pray,

Approach Him with love and boldness, come out of the fray.

Watch as He sleeps in heavenly peace,

Put your hand in His and be at ease.

Find rest for your soul, whosoever you may be!!

HOPE AND PEACE TO YOU, HAVE A BLESSED CHRISTMAS

In the Garden

The pain, the agony, the oppression Jesus faced in the garden.

Not my will but Yours be done, as He looked up,

There was no other way, so He drank from the cup.

The soldiers came and took Him to a mock trial,

They beat Him and whipped Him and spewed all that was vile.

When Love came to town, it was a chilly night.

Soldiers came to arrest Him; His friends all took flight from fright.

This was the hour for which He had come,

To pay the wages of sin, it was a great sum.

He was to be the sacrifice Lamb,

The place of the skull was where His death took place,

O, the man of sorrow, that look on His face.

"Father, forgive them, for they do not know what they do."[4]

We are all sinners, He died in the place of me, and you too.

The earth grew dark for three hours, in the midday sun,

---

[4] Luke 23:34

The earth roared and quaked at the death of Gods only Son.

"It is finished"[5], He said with His last breath,

They stuck a spear in His side, of His death to be sure,

Out flowed blood and water, which can cleanse to your core.

His body lay in a rich man's tomb, for three days He was there.

This man named Jesus, the King of the Jews,

He can be your King too, if you so choose.

The resurrection radiance on that morning
when an angel rolled away the stone,

Jesus walked out of the tomb with a gigantic smile,

With great joy at accomplishing what He came to earth for.

With His winning victory over death, a
reconciling new covenant to be sure.

He came to destroy the devil's work and to seek and save the lost,

He seeks to find and set them free, at such a high cost.

The resurrection hope and light go forth
to a world held in darkness.

Without hope, how does one cope?

His love is beyond comprehension,

---

[5] John 19:30

Whether you're rich or poor,

Whether life is good, or has become such a chore,

There is One who loves you more!

To reconcile to God there is provided only one way,

Only by the high price that Jesus did pay.

Your biggest life decision is whether to
make Jesus your Savior and Lord,

To live life without Him, no man can afford.

The gift of salvation is yours, If Jesus you choose,

To reject God's gift, you're the one to lose.

I've tasted and seen that the Lord, He is so good!

Solace

Jesus is the rock,

He's the guardian Shepherd of His flock.

He rules and reigns with kindness and care,

He makes it so we can live with no fear. He
wipes away and dries every tear.

Someday, when the trumpet does sound,

In the clouds He will appear.

If you feel bogged down and your life is in a pit,

If you feel like life has become a mess,

Humble yourself, go to God, repent, and your sins to Him confess.

Some have lost their way and ability to
smile, go to God and reconcile.

I would rather not walk another mile,

With those on the wide road, rank and file.

There is a path which leads to life,

Go to the Shepherd with all your sorrow and strife.

The most broken soul, He can restore.

Salvation's a gift for the rich or the poor.

Some apples are rotten, right to the core,

Not too hard for Jesus to restore.

God seen all human history, and you're
not the nut too hard to crack,

Turn to the Lord, and don't look back!

Seek the Lord while He may be found.

Don't fall for satans lies and tricks and be one of the bound.

I once was lost, but now I am found.

Get quiet and listen to silence sound surround.

Reflect on truth and let life into your heart cascade,

Stop digging the hole and put down the spade.

Thy word is truth, and knowing truth brings liberty and peace,

The victory is won, the battles shall cease.

Resurrection power rose Jesus from the dead.

He has become the lifter of my head.

He's my Savior and King, a new song I do sing.

I trust in the Lord; His words call me blessed.

God's word now lights up my life's path.

Jesus came to find the lost,

He goes for the one, and He paid the high cost.

If that one, is you to find eternal life,

Be thankful to escape with your life from the strife.

We will never fully comprehend the depth of God's love.

So glad I'm a citizen of His kingdom above,

The Holy Spirit is our Helper, He descended like a dove.

I humbly acknowledge Jesus as Sovreign King and Lord.

I hold up the shield of faith and wield God's word as a sword.

My life, I pray, is a fragrant aroma, as I speak of the gospel Hope,

To say, "nope" would be the decision of the devil's dope.

A fool says to himself, "there is no God."

Off to a godless life many do plod.

When life's last breath comes for us all,

May you be one that did heed Jesus' call.

My Turn to Dance

O to be led by the blind,

With one act of compassion to learn next
time to step up and be kind.

He stood on the side, stunned and confused.

The world around sounds like it's going so fast.

He's unsure where to go,

Unsure how to go with the flow.

He lives in a world of darkness, there is no light.

From that day in his past, he was robbed of his sight.

There have been many hurdles he has jumped,

He needs the help of a stranger, to no longer be stumped.

A fast car pulls up out of its stride,

One who's book cover should not be read,

He lends himself, so the blind could be led.

Now on the other side safe and thankful, the
blind man says, "thanks, and goodbye!"

I pull up my car to the fast car driver, I look over inside.

Thankful in this world which goes so fast, he did
not leave the man stranded in time,

He took a moment to be so kind.

Next time, I'll get my chance,

I pray to be ready for when it's my turn to dance.

Sunset Beach

Sitting on the beach feeling the breeze,

The people are silhouettes against the sea.

The gulls ride the wind as they dart and tease,

Suns going down, another day flees.

The sand is white, the palms are green,

Hints of pink in the sky, reflecting on clouds and vast ocean.

There goes the sun,

Going down but not with a frown.

I'm sitting with a smile,

As I sit and enjoy the evening sky for a while.

Some are still in the water swimming; the
buoys bounce with the waves coming in.

A band plays a colorful song in the distance,

The colors I'm seeing bring the tune some fame.

I sit in silence with awe,

As the gull filled sky is without a flaw.

Another beautiful sky, silently pointing
to the glory of the Most High.

The Wind That Blew

Does anyone know from where it comes?

I was on a balcony in Haiti when the trees started to sway.

A game of cards we just finished to play.

We walked to the rail and the wind came in with a swoosh.

Suddenly, the trees bending, shimmy and shake, and even the bush.

Now I hear the sound of much needed rain.

The farmers go to bed with a smile, cause
the ground had been in pain.

The dry crusted earth really needed a drink,

Now there's enough water to fill even the kitchen sink.

God knows where it comes from, I don't need to know.

Just as He knows how His Spirit does flow.

We say, "Come Holy Spirit, breathe on us we pray.

Blow in like the wind and on the thirsty soul we say.

Come Holy Spirit, wash the soul in pain,

Come Holy Spirit, bring your reign."

Freedom

I've lived a life that knew no peace.

The endless pain, I felt it would never cease.

To have no hope and many a care.

Sometimes I would just sit with a blank gaunt stare.

I searched the lows with the highs to try and get some relief.

I allowed myself to be robbed of my belief.

Life was not meant to live as a slave,

Or to live like Legion who lived in a cave.

My shovel dug deep for the pit I lived in,

Now I put my shovel down and I'm ready
to have Jesus deal with my sin.

He said, "I've come to set the captive free."

For that reason of love, He let Himself be killed on that tree.

There was no other way, He drank from the cup.

He is the lifter of my head and now I can look up.

He arose from the dead and in that is my hope.

To the way I once lived I now can say, "NOPE!!!"

In the center of His will is where I choose to live.

By His grace I stand, with the freedom He does give.

Love from Above

The world is fallen!

Many have woes,

Some say, "It's just how life goes."

Just another day,

Gotta go to work and get some pay.

The years fly by, life goes by so fast.

Some are rich, some poor,

Some think life is one big chore.

Others think life is just a bore.

Some's experience leaves them sour and sore.

Some have come to find peace beyond measure,

Life's memories and moments made; a joy filled hearts treasure.

Some just keep going from empty pleasure to pleasure.

There are two roads in life, one wide; one narrow.

On the narrow, of much more worth than many a sparrow,

On the wide they go in and out with the tide.

They go with the flow, wherever they go.

Truth does prevail and pierces the heart.

Makes you question, where did life start?

To question life's meaning is a good question to have.

If we search, with all our heart, Truth we will surely find,

Our eyes are fixed on Him from above, promised peace of mind,

Life in Jesus far exceeds walking blind.

I have been low down and in despair,

There is One, who is the lifter of my head and gives me hope,

To reject Jesus, I'd have to be a dope.

Borderline

Here, on a bench, I am sitting on the border,

Blue sky reflects on the sea.

One of those days with a sunny ocean breeze.

People walking nervously, trying to avoid the sneeze.

Orange arrow on the sidewalk tells you on which side to walk,

They painted it on, they should have used chalk.

We all want this virus to leave quick,

It's been a pain in the butt, like to give it a good swift kick.

Moored boats in the harbor, bobbing to the breakers,

Be nice to sail away, got any takers?

People out walking, enjoying their day,

Saw a circle in the field, an outdoor meeting of A.A.

Some stay sober, but a lot of people hurting
and some choose to break out and use,

With a virus in town some lives have burnt a fuse.

Powers gone out; low down despair,

Good to get out and get some fresh air.

Some stay in and develop a blank stare,

That's not healthy, thankful there's a God that does care.

I look up and see a gull fly in like a dove,

Like the Spirit flew down to pour out His power and love.

Time to get the fuse re-booted. Let's try a new course.

Time to go to the power Source.

God wants to heal our very soul,

To bring health to our lives and make us whole.

He wants for us to make the move,

As we draw near, away goes fear.

As we draw near, He wipes away every tear.

As we draw near, He bears all our care.

As we draw near, to know Him, we discover the gift of eternal life.

As we draw near.... He draws near.

I sit here with the ocean breeze, with the
Sons light shining brightly on me.

Thankful for the Helpers power!

Father's helping this very hour.

I look out at the vast depths, but nothing
compares to the vast depths of His love.

No more sitting on the border.

We are crossing over to be a son or a daughter.

Going for the Hope who is the anchor of my soul.

Despair can be as dark as Sheol.

Light has come, come Spirit hover.

Hence,

It is time to get off the fence.

Hopeful, many will believe and repent,

Humble ourselves before the One heaven Sent.

Encounters

I, Zaccheus, climbed upon that tree,

To catch a glimpse of that Man walking towards me.

He changed my life, forever set free.

In my mother's womb, I jumped and leapt,

At the presence of the One being formed as He slept.

There were three wise men who traveled so far,

To behold the King of all kings, they were led by a star.

I've sat here for years, a beggar was me,

Till I had the encounter, now my blind eyes see.

My friend was deaf, he couldn't hear a thing,

Now he loves to hear people sing.

My skin was leprous, along with the nine,

I returned to thank Him, cause now I am fine.

I was caught in my sin and thrown to the floor,

In His eyes was love and compassion as
He spoke, "Go and sin no more."[6]

---

[6] John 8:11b

I've been dead four days, my body does stink,

I heard my name called, my eyes opened in a blink.

The news went around, He's the One in whom to believe,

I don't care who you are, Sally, Sue, Fred or Steve.

On bended knee beside my bed,

With all reverence, I bowed my head.

He purchased our freedom with His blood on that tree,

With mercy and grace, salvation is a gift for free.

The Prince of peace loves us all so much,

Reach out in prayer, encounter His loving touch.

O to be forgiven, washed white as snow,

He responds to whosoever, His eyes peeled to and fro.

He lavishes His grace unto the humble of heart,

So thankful to be part of the family, it's
what I looked for and sought.

Thank you Jesus for encountering me,

And for dying on calvary, so we could be set free.

My friend spent his days not able to speak,

Now it's as though he has sprung a leak.

He pours out the good news and shouts from the roof tops,

He doesn't care if you call the cops.

News is so good you can't keep it inside.

I pray someday, in Him you will learn to abide.

New Shoe

All things new,

I will walk in a new shoe.

Which way do I go? High or low, in the heat or snow?

FIRE!!!

I want to go in the flow of the way the Spirits wind blows.

No one knows from where it comes or to where it goes.

Here I set in the city.

Somewhere someone is laughing, someone witty.

Somewhere there is someone sitting alone in the cold.

There is someone brooding, festering in a sad life's mold.

Mold which grows and festers and spores.

Lives become a dredge, like doing chores.

Someone wants to set you free,

That one gave His life on the tree.

The possessed and oppressed, His truth sets them free.

Someone asks me, "how are you?"

They tell me, "Your face seems a wee bit blue, you
look like someone, who needs a new shoe."

I take aim to take a shot at life, and I can't hit the cue.

Is this all there is? It can't be true.

To some life seems to be a hit and a miss.

There are some, seem to be at peace, and all is bliss.

What do some have that they appear not to be lost?

I'm told I can be found too; the price is …..... no cost.

They tell me about life's greatest gift.

My head facing down, could definitely use a lift.

No more, "Why are you cast down, O my soul?"[7]

He lifts my head out of the depths of deaths hold.

The warmth of LOVES breath, melts hearts grown frigidly cold.

I tell you a new way to go, a love walk, that will knock off your sock.

I fix my eyes on the Savior, that will finish my faith story.

Each new day ahead, till I breathe my last and enter into glory.

Some day we will join those already passed.

The anchor of hope is real,

---

[7] Psalm 42:5

I implore all to close the deal.

Receive the free gift, that cost such a price.

Bought with the Son of man's blood sacrifice.

Believe and repent, let the truth set you free.

Discover redemption at the foot of the tree.

Put your hand in the hand of the Man that walked on the sea.

He's the beginning and the end, and He calls me friend.

So, if your life is askew,

Let Jesus give you a new shoe too!!!

Looking for Me

The day they came for me,

I was so young and carefree.

I had my whole life ahead,

Now the minutes tick by, in this life of dread.

I was caught in the lie of a friendly, hello,

But I was dealing with beasts that were far from mellow.

I lie in this bed, inside I feel dead.

Now they have me hooked on the drugs that I crave,

They're the only relief I find as they send in another depraved.

This vicious cycle of misery and pain,

The hope I held out seems to be all in vain.

I'm tormented and naked; Am I losing my mind?

Pull it together....someday, freedom I'll find.

The hope I hold out, again, turns to despair.

Sometimes, I wish my end was near.

Does anybody out there really care?

Do they know I'm still alive?

Are they looking for me?

Will I again someday be free?

Time has stopped ticking: existence is darkness and gloom.

As more and more enter and leave my room,

each one takes another little piece of my soul,

Now I feel like the walking dead, and life has become dark like coal.

Will I, one day, ever again, feel whole?

Darkness.......Turmoil.......and fear, so dead inside, I can't shed a tear.

Again, I hope for the end to draw near.

Numbness, misery and pain; I feel I must be going insane.

Once I was so young and so carefree,

I need an escape.... Is that drink for me?

The booze, the drugs, being used; that's my life now.

I'm a slave, a prisoner, inside and out.

My life goes on, in the daily dredge.

I wish someone would break down the door who carries a big sledge.

Instead, there is One, with a still quiet knock.

You can hear it if you're listening, don't be
among those who would mock.

He is the One who hung upon calvary's tree,

He knows how to set the captives free.

He will come to you gently, humble and kind,

Even when you feel like you're going out of your mind.

He holds out to you, His nail pierced hand.

Go ahead take it; He is the only hope in all the land.

I know it is hard for you to trust,

In Him if you hope, your chains He will bust.

No longer a captive, inside your set free.

I've discovered that Someone was looking for me.

Big C

I sit and ponder, of days gone yonder.

Of love I knew, of those still true,

But some I feel blue.

When I was a boy,

I sat on my dad's knee,

He who's the head of our family tree.

We weren't poor, but we were rich in other ways,

I do remember but with a little haze.

I've been told I have the Big C,

Which has taken many members of our family tree.

I've already gone many rounds, and the final bell will soon sound.

I want to fight, but be at peace, but this
life will soon give up its lease.

My body withers and I feel some pain, but
I look forward to the life I'll gain.

I'll say goodbye to this earthly tent, and my
spirit will soon soar, heaven bent.

My Lord said He goes to prepare a place for
me in the mansion with many rooms,

He calls those who are His, right out of their tombs.

I've heard healing is possible for me, as I make a plea.

When my time comes, there's a place made for me, I can hardly
wait to see, but I am torn for there are those I leave behind,

There are ties that bind.

And for those I am sad, there are those
that knew me when I was a lad.

There are those I hope to see before it's too
late, who knows why they are sore?

In the big scheme of things, forgiveness should spread to our core.

Remember we are cut from the same cloth,

Haven't we given enough to eat to the moth?

Whatever divides, let it melt, and remember
the close feelings once to be felt.

God help us to communicate before the clock
ticks, and time tells us it's too late.

Have no fear, I'll see you there.

Walking through the pearly gate.

America

In God we trust,

I've come to know this is a must!

Land of the free, home of the brave,

What have your people come to crave?

E-pluribus Unum, but some want to divide us...out of many one,

Do our people still seek the Son?

You can't fool God, He's not easy to con.

Forgive us God, your heart is torn,

We have strayed a long way from when this nation was born.

We have strayed from our nation's original intent,

Many on a different path, bound for hell.

Forgotten.... Jesus the Son, heaven sent.

God bless America, the country that I love!

We must pray, and turn from our wicked way,

YOU will hear from heaven and heal our land
as we come together as one to pray.

Our people who number the grains of the beaches
sand, are now in a state of decay.

One heart at a time YOU can re-generate and renew.

Open the door, Holy One and let the river flow, Holy
Spirit come as the dove who once flew.

Holy Spirit, come help us, and let your fire burn,

As one by one we humbly repent and to the Lord return.

To God who loves us more than we know,

He wants to encase us in His light aglow.

Thank YOU for your kindness, YOUR mercy and grace,

One day we will see You face to face.

Those of us who believe and received Jesus YOUR Son,

We are cleansed and holy, may we be united as one.

God looks for the heart completely His, that He
might strengthen and support them,

May we be desperate for God, like the women
that reached for Jesus' garment hem.

God, we desperately need you, that is for sure,

Let's turn unto Jesus, whether rich or poor!

We look to the cross all across our land,

Be you one of many grains of sand.

We run to the shelter of the Most High, our lives in YOUR hand,

So go ahead and strike up the band,

And sing the song all through this land.

We desperately need YOU God, in this land that we love!

"God Bless America!!!"

Sweet Streams

Mountain views all around,

Driving cross country, westward bound.

Listen really close, you'll hear the still sound,

The peaceful quiet stillness, of one once lost, but found.

Sun shines bright, from daybreak to twilight,

Clouds burst forth red, a sight delight.

The beautiful day comes to night.

Stars in the countryside shine so bright.

Tonight's moon is only a sliver,

Out too long gazing, starting to shiver.

The stars form their shapes; there's the big dipper.

It guided many a ship, many skippers.

I think I'll go in the cabin, get changed and throw on my slippers.

I'll get a rip roaring fire going in the pot belly stove.

Get it going so hot, red cherry glow,

Time to let my head hit the pillow.

I'll wake in the morning and see what I can see.

Maybe a New Mexico elk, but they so easily flee.

I'll take a walk down to the streamside tree.

Sitting against the tree, pondering how I've been set free.

Wasted so much of life going astray, in the
green pasture is where I want to lay.

So good to get away from the city fray.

Stream bellows out a real sweet sound,

Blessed sounds of nature, so good to be found.

I hear the sound of a bird's flapping wings, He lands
above in the tree and starts to chirping and sings.

Warm sunshine on my face, what a nice day! A
couple of squirrels run by, they like to play.

I open my bible and dwell in a psalm, The Lords
word uplifts me, and keeps me calm.

Tin Roof

Sitting under a Honduran grape tree, with
a beautiful view of the sea.

Shaded from the hot sun, equipping pastors
so more lost souls can be won.

Pastors come from around the region,
around 20, not a whole legion.

Pastor Greg spoke from his heart, speaking
of love and freedom from sin.

The deep cleansing ministry of Holy Spirit,

A white gleaming robe, all who are His shall wear it.

Those who submit to our loving and merciful God.

Those who've been washed in the blood of the Lamb.

We are called to be a royal priesthood,
rescued from darkness to light,

We are seated with Him in heavenly places,

called from many different tribes and races.

As the Spirit moved and flowed, and the Word
was shared that we could be sanctified.

All's going well, as the heavens turned grey,

The sky began to rumble,

We entered the unfinished church without a stumble.

Just as the last pastor stepped through the door,
the skies opened up and it began to pour.

It rained so hard, you couldn't hear yourself the think,

Way more rain than to fill a kitchen sink.

The crowd began to worship in spirit and in truth.

The clapping, guitar, and singing was filling the air,

We prayed for those burdened by carrying their cross.

We knocked on the door of heaven with all supplication,

Heaven knocked back on our tin roof, with jubilation.

It was a time of worship we will all remember.

So glad in the family of God, I'm a member.

As we ended with more words of truth,

May all pastors stick together, just like Naomi and Ruth.

What Are You Trippin'?

I'm told a trip starts with a step,

Some have fear and ran out of pep.

Some have through time, chosen to be frozen.

I'm so glad I chose to let God restore my soul and make me whole.

He restored my ability to choose,

So, I don't continue to lose.

The way I was living was taking its toll,

There was a time I would wake and bake and smoke a bowl.

The life I was living became empty and dry,

Many awake at the break of dawn with a sigh.

Another day of the same old stuff,

Some check out early, they've had enough.

There are different ways to get comfortably numb,

Some choices I made; boy was I dumb.

Orange sunshine, blotter, green tic, purple microdot,

In the seventies, you could do drugs, or not.

You could take a trip without leaving home, as someone once said,

I would get so wasted, so glad I'm not dead.

The trips I took left me dead inside,

So glad Jesus found me, and now in Him I have learned to abide.

Wherever you're at, on your journey through life,

Tired of the stress, or emptiness, maybe some strife?

Maybe life is good, but sometimes you feel hollow.

There is only One that is a jolly good Fellow and is worthy to follow.

Life without Jesus, whether rich or poor, can leave you hollow.

Some prodigal years I left the path of life
after ten years of my twenties.

I found new ways to get a stash, I turned my back on the Rock,

I delved into the foolish rock of cocaine, I'm
fortunate I did not go insane.

I was so lost and drank myself silly at many a bash.

Although there is some pleasure in sin,

It's only for a season, then much more empty within.

There's a God shaped hole in our soul,

Which can only be filled with God's love, to be made whole.

So thankful for the vastness and depth of God's love,

He showed me mercy and grace, from His throne above.

I searched many highs, but just got low.

Dug down deeper in the pit, I would go.

I'm so glad God didn't give up on me, and my life He just shelved.

Instead, He showered me with mercy and grace,

Holy Spirit helped me to get back into the race.

Someday we'll all see Him face to face.

Thankful, for the blood of Jesus shed on the cross.

All sin God can erase.

I've been clean and sober for twenty one years,

God knows how to wipe away our tears.

To some, the gospels good news has them slinging jeers,

The look on some faces is frowning and sneers.

When your journey and trip through life
comes to the end of your years,

When it's your turn to take your last breath.

Only one thing will matter,

And you'll be glad you read all this chatter.

I've journeyed and taken many trips in my life.

I've seen India and the life of poverty some live.

I've seen Rome, and Florence and right down the
grand canal of Venice, that floated my boat.

Been through the streets of London, seen
the Queens palace and crown jewels,

But without God in my life, I could be counted among the fools.

A fool has said in his heart, "there is no God."[8]

I've known sorrow and sadness which can come in like a flood.

I took a trip to relieve the pain, but I never did yet make it to Spain.

I've been to Honduras, Costa Rica, Mexico and Belize.

I've climbed Mayan pyramids and walked on their ancient ground.

Most important of all.... I'm so glad for the
love of God that I have found.

I've gone to Haiti to share the love of God, some
are steeped in voodoo and are so blind,

Many did not know the love of God; and that He is so kind.

I've seen cities and oceans, mountains, rivers and lakes.

I've met people who are real, and some who are fakes.

---

[8] Psalm 14:1a

I've seen people living in dumps among the burning trash,

They live off the garbage, strapped for cash.

I've been to some jungles to share the good news,

Seen people lifted out of their blues,

By Jesus, the King of the Jews.

I went to Israel a couple times and saw where Jesus walked,

Saw the city He grew up in, abide in the vine.

I've been on the Mount of Beatitudes where Jesus did speak,

He spoke to the poor, the humble and to the meek.

I swam in the sea of Galilee, so glad I put my hand
in the hand of the Man who stilled the water.

I've seen the Holy sites, and the place of the skull,
Golgotha, where they crucified my Lord.

satan thought he brought an end to Jesus' life journey....

Glad to see the Garden of Gethsemane, where
Jesus made a plea to not drink the cup.

So glad He said, "Not My will but Yours be
done."[9] To His loving Father above.

Jesus died a brutal death to pay the price on the cross,

---

[9] Luke 22:42b

The devil was mistaken, it was not a loss.

Jesus suffered, bled, died and was put in a rich man's tomb,

Three days later, He rose from the dead in resurrection power.

They built a cathedral above the tomb where He was laid,

A path for reconciliation with God has been made.

A new covenant was made with the blood of the Lamb.

All the worldwide over, people worship and sing,

"All glory and honor and praise to our King."

In my life's journeys of places and thoughts, I have found,

Only One has the way to truth and life that is sound.

No matter where your trips have taken you,
there is hope eternal extended as a gift.

You may be rich and snooty, you may be a bit sappy,

Heck you may be slap happy.

You may be fearful and empty, sorrowful or blue,

You don't have to listen to me or take my cue.

Please believe me when I say,

The good news, Jesus' gospel, is the only true way.

Let His truth cut to your soul and spirit like a knife.

Read the Holy Bible, receive the good news I pray,

Come to faith and believe, have a change
of heart and turn from your way.

Jesus' truth is the only way provided out of the fray.

With Holy Spirits help, learn to abide in and be a follower of HIM.

Jesus the Messiah, God's only provision of hope for this world.

So, I'm not trippin, but I am on a journey,

I'll still be abiding in Him when my body is wheeled out on a gurney.

When it appears to be my life journey end, don't be fooled.

I go to meet the beginning and the end, the Alpha and the Omega.

The best is yet to come when my short earthly sojourn is over,

Oh, what a trip that will be,

To meet the One, who died on that tree, to set you and me FREE,

Free to enter and drink from the River of Life.

And the Spirit and the bride say, "Come!" And let him who hears
say, "Come!" And let him who thirsts come. Whoever desires, let
him take the water of life freely. {Revelation 22:17}

Vanishing Vapor

Time flies,

Like a blink of your eyes.

By the time this poem is read,

How many will be found dead?

At your life's end,

I pray Jesus is your friend.

A Savior into this world God did send,

He lived and died and rose and did ascend.

The Son returned to heaven above,

From whence God's Spirit descended as a Dove.

God Almighty is Love.

In this life we will have trials and trouble,

Unless you live your life in a bubble.

There is an anchor for your soul,

There is a way to be made whole.

Some are afflicted by evil so vile,

Some have lost the ability to smile.

If you're broken, hurt and lost,

Turn to the One who paid the ultimate cost.

Some want all of life's strife to cease,

May I introduce you to the Prince of peace.

He is Immanuel, God with us,

Some use His name as a swear word and cuss.

He is the King of kings, and Lord of lords.

The Shepherd of my soul,

The One who made me whole.

Know Him when you're the one for whom the bell does toll!

King Jesus

Sick of the Poop, I'm Flying My Coop

I've heard of birds that have flown the coop,
but here I stand upon my stoop.

The cage is open, I can sense the breeze,

To fly away I could do with such ease.

It all looks and feels a little scary out there.

What am I to do with all my anxiety and fear?

I'd love to go through life without shedding a tear.

To learn to overcome all my fear,

Can't stop thinking of snare after snare,

There is something waiting to get me out there,

Out there where all is unsure, with fright I shake to my core.

Till one night in the Un-comfort of my darkness,

The voice within tells me to drop my knees to the floor.

I talk to the Maker of all that is seen and unseen, He
lets me know He loves me and thinks I am keen.

I'm able to cast upon Him all my cares,
and He takes away all my fears.

When I crawl back up to step on my stoop,
I realize I am so sick of the poop.

Something real has happened inside; I have faith
to believe that in Him I will learn to abide.

I turn as I have a thousand times before;
the cage is open as a door,

What's imprisoned me, will no more.

Nobody knows where the wind comes from, but I spread
my wings and find the unction to soar through the
door. No looking back to those days under attack.

I soar on ahead; from the past I have fled.

The sky is beautiful, with clouds bright white,
even with the sun, O what a sight.

I really love the freedom I've found; I will never
again allow myself to be bound,

Living one day at a time with the hope I have found,

Next time you hear a bird chirping in the
morning, realize it's a song of freedom,

I too join in to sing to the King of all Kings,
and it is sweet music to His ears.

Rest

Basking in the sunlight of His presence.

To my core shines the warmth of peace,

The brightness, the wars in my mind shall cease.

I look to the one who restores my soul,

He is the author and finisher of faith; I fix
my eyes on Him towards the goal.

I sit at His feet, and lean on the tree,

This is the tree where I am set free.

No more shadow living, with darkness and woe,

A new life to live, and new seeds to sow.

The warmth, as I bask, melts away shivers,

My best efforts at wholeness and warmth brought only slivers.

Of hope and love, joy, and rest.

At peace with the Savior is where I am blessed.

So, I am trading my sorrows, all darkness and pain,

To bask in His Sonlight, 'til He brings His reign.

Look Around

Look up at the sky so blue, saw an eagle soar, away he flew.

So many songbirds dart and weave,

They flock together in a row on a wire,

A beautiful sight to admire.

I hear them chirp, they sing with glee,

At the sight of the cat, they flee for the tree.

Sky so vast with big puffy cloud,

As I stare in wonder, city sounds, not so loud.

Suns on the way to its chamber, with colorful sight,

A treat for the eyes, sunset delight.

As dusk rolls forth its colorful hues,

Yellows, red, pink, orange, awesome night views.

Gives way to the darkness with a sliver of
moon; starry night shining so bright.

I saw a falling star plummet the expanse,

All part of the creators choreographed dance.

Light years away, in my mind the moment stands still,

Enjoy moments like these, times not to kill.

Enjoy every moment, time does not stand still.

Another day has come and gone, enjoy
the night sky's beautiful song.

The beauty orchestrated as a beautiful melody,
God's creation song for you and for me.

The darkest part of the night is just before dawn,

As I'm amazed by the starry night sky, I'm laid out on the lawn.

An idea comes to me, I'll go to the beach,

The suns coming up with beauty to beseech.

The horizon on the water starts to flicker with light,

The crest of the sun beams forth, goodbye night.

The clouds and the sky start to reflect the glory,

As creation shouts of the King of kings unspoken story.

Awesome colors fill the morning sky,

The Master painter brings a tear to my eye.

The gulls fly and ride the ocean's breeze,

Sunrise is a moment to seize.

Some people jog, and walking the beach at the
water's edge, a walk does the heart good.

"What an awesome day!", to the passerby with a smile,

I think I'll seek seashells for a while.

Every shell is different, like a fingerprint or snowflake,

What a wonderful creation our Maker did make.

I think I'll go back to the house for a nice slab of chocolate cake.

As I drift off to sleep realizing life is no dress rehearsal,

Lord I want to know you more!

From my wrong ways, with Your help, there will be a reversal.

Oh, what You have planned for those who are Yours, one
day we'll view the unfathomable kingdom of Yours.

Goodnight, Lord, I say with a smile,

I look forward to walking with you, one
step at a time till my last mile.

Virus

I wish this virus from my memory could erase.

But It's here and has yet to cease to exist.

What a blow to the whole human race.

The invisible enemy comes in like a flood.

You can't feel it, or sense it, but it's real just the same,

Is it natural, or is there someone to blame?

People are told to stay at home, the entire
world has come to a stop.

Some venture out to walk or roam.

To feel the sun, see the blue sky, smell the fresh
air. See the waves crash, or flowers grow.

Some choose to stay inside to sit and stare,

At the four walls, how much more could we bear?

I hope they come to know the kindness of God, He is love,

He's the One enthroned above.

Some look down in deep dark despair,

They look at you sideways with a distraught leer.

Some are having a hard time to cope,

Maybe not realizing there is One in which to put their hope.

Some sit around smoking their dope,

That's how they cope.

Some get higher than a kite,

Some have drinks and get really tight.

Some get the bad news, that their loved one has died!

A slap across the face, emotions can't hide.

There has been many a tear,

The media blitz keeps many in fear.

Some wear a mask to protect from the germ,

Some go outside like there's no hint of concern.

Some put on the N-95,

Because they want to stay alive.

Some choose to drink from a glass, and
some sit and drink the whole cask.

Some go through life so empty inside,

Drowned sorrows, behind a mask to hide.

To some, life is one big party which never ends,

Till the lights go out and the music stops,
heart beats its last beat....

Our turn will come to have a toe tag on our feet.

So glad, at the foot of the Cross, all my sins and sorrow I did cast.

One day I'll stand before Jesus, the King of kings I will meet,

So glad there's a wedding feast and Jesus
invites me to take a seat.

Some choose to stay outside the white pearly gate,

Someday, like Noah's day, the door will shut, and it will be too late.

There's a gift of grace offered to all,

Some, by their own choice, refuse to heed the call.

When death is so rampant, it makes you think,

This short life could be over in just an eye blink.

Jesus wants to save your soul,

Some just sit and smoke another bowl.

Some live their lives and in their Christmas stocking there's coal.

God loves you and wants to give you a clean slate,

For some the hour is getting late.

Let God wash your sins away, white as snow.

The Savior died on the cross in my place,

So, I could know Him and one day see Him face to face.

The Lambs book of Life is where I want to see your name,

Be you rich or poor, humble or of great fame.

To save your soul, the choice is yours,

The invites are out, come one and all,

We all suffer the results of the great fall.

You need a Savior, that's for sure.

All of our apples are rotten to the core.

This virus will one day be a thing of the past,

Peace unto you and to all the faces downcast.

Knock While It Can Still Be Opened

"I go to prepare a place for you."

A promise from One who can make you anew.

We live in a world with darkness and pain,

One went to the Place of the Skull, He without blemish or stain.

The only man-made thing in heaven is
from the marks of that cross,

On the body of the Savior who appeared to suffer such a loss.

The wounds to His hands, and the holes in His feet,

As He hung there so many thoughts that He suffered defeat.

There were few present that darkened day, which shed a tear,

There were many stirred to hatred and growled with a vile snare,

Man made a fifth hole in heaven, the wound in His side,

Where the soldier stuck Him with a spear,

Out came the flow of water and blood, as the haters did leer.

Saviors redeeming power, to lift humanity from the muck and mire.

They took the Saviors body to a rich man's grave,

It was His death the haters did crave.

His brutalized body lay there while the tomb
entrance rolled closed with a stone,

His body lay there, stone cold, dead to the bone.

He made a promise, and He doesn't lie,

"I will rise from the dead, when my body does die."

His followers hid out, cowering in fear,

Three days later, one came with spices, for His body to care,

WHAT??? The stone rolled away, and inside she did stare.

There were two angels sitting where Jesus' body had laid.

They said, "Why do you seek the living among the dead?"[10]

The Savior has risen in resurrection power,

He's the One the world needs to look to, at this very hour,

This is not time to snare or be sour,

Jesus wants to be our strong tower.

He's Gods only answer to man's sin sorrowing fall.

The good news goes out to everyone and to all.

It's your choice to have this hope, as an anchor for your souls,

---

[10] Luke 24:5b

Especially good news to the one for whom the bell tolls.

There was a huge price paid for the redemption of man.

He gave His all, so we could be saved and restored.

If we humble ourselves at the cross, repent
and draw near to the Lord.

The devil is a liar, out to rob, kill and destroy.

There's a soul battle being waged, and the free will choice is yours,

To have renewed strength and mount up as an eagle who soars,

Or to be in outer darkness, FOREVER CLOSED DOORS.

Final thoughts, warnings and encouragement from God's word, which is like a GPS system for us in this mortal life. Knowledge of God's word brings freedom. All scripture references are from the New King James version of the Holy Bible.

I hope you have enjoyed the poems I have shared. It is so important to approach our relationship with God with uncomplicated simplicity and childlike innocence and trust, as we learn to grow in our relationship with God. Always remember that "God is love"[11]. God loves us beyond what we will ever be able to fully comprehend.

Jesus said, "And you shall know the truth, and the truth shall make you free."[12] It is important to know that in this world, we have a spiritual enemy that is out to destroy us. The devil deals in accusations and lies and makes us self-condemn ourselves with guilt and shame. He tries to keep people in fear, despair and hopelessness. Jesus conquered and destroyed the enemy through His death on the cross, burial, and resurrection three days later when Jesus rose from the dead. It's good to get to know Jesus, the One that overcame death because we all will get our turn to breathe our last breath. Through knowledge of the bible scriptures, we discover truth which sets us free to hope, "hope we have as an anchor of the soul."[13] Discover the help and power available to us through the Christian life with the help of the Helper, the promised Holy Spirit who empowers us to walk by the Spirit and not after the flesh. There is a big difference between the devils' accusations and condemnation aiming to beat us down, and the Holy Spirit who will convict us of sin and woo us with love and kindness to get us to respond to grace and have a change of heart

---

[11] 1 John 4:8
[12] John 8:32
[13] Hebrews 6:19

and mind and turn from the wide path which leads to destruction and instead choosing to walk through life on the narrow path of life empowered by the Dunamis power of the Holy Spirit.

Location, location, location.... prepare for the eternal destination of your soul. Jesus said, "I am the way, the truth, and the life. No one comes to the Father except through Me."[14] Some people think that when you die you automatically go to heaven. That is not true because we are all sinners, and fall short, and sin does not enter a holy awesome God's presence. God longs to extend grace - (unmerited favor and love of God) and mercy, even to the worst of us sinners, but many people will not humble themselves before our kind and loving God and turn from their sins and let Jesus sit on the throne of their life. This causes God's grace to be unable to flow into a life. Some people reject the whole idea of God. God will not override your free will choice of whether to receive Him or reject Him. "And this is the testimony; that God has given us eternal life, and this life is in His Son. He who has the Son has life; he who does not have the Son of God does not have life."[15]

Eternal life is a gift from God that needs to be received. It's a matter of believing by faith in the good news of the gospel of Jesus Christ, and repentance- (TURNING FROM SIN, HAVING A CHANGE OF HEART AND MIND, AND TURNING TO HIM) turning from a path of sin which has the penalty of death. I am very grateful that Jesus took the penalty for sin upon Himself. He died in our place. Jesus allowed Himself to be brutally beaten, whipped and hung on the cross so that through the blood which He shed; a new blood covenant was made to reconcile us to God. He sacrificed Himself to be the propitiation for mankind's fallen sin

---

[14] John 14:6
[15] 1 John 5:11,12

nature, making it possible for whosoever would choose to receive the gift of salvation. Jesus, the Messiah, is, "the Lamb of God who takes away the sin of the world."[16] The choice of whether to receive or reject the gift of salvation is the most important decision anyone can make in their lifetime. A decision of eternal consequence, seek the Lord, because nobody is guaranteed tomorrow.

"For the wages of sin is death, but the gift of God is eternal life in Christ Jesus our Lord."[17] Don't be fooled or deceived, when people die, they don't turn into a new angel that God needed, and they don't automatically enter into heaven. There is a Lambs book of life with names entered into it, of those who have been "born again" Jesus said, "unless one is born again, he cannot see the kingdom of God."[18]

People that have repented of sin and have received the gift of eternal life offered by God and have come into a covenant with God through the precious blood of Jesus Christ. They have had their dead fallen spirit regenerated and made alive and sealed with God's precious Holy Spirit. The bible encourages these newborn babes in the faith to feed themselves spiritually, "as newborn babes, desire the pure milk of the word, that you may grow thereby, if indeed you have tasted that the Lord is gracious."[19]

Read your Bibles people! If you have one, take it off the shelf, if you don't have one, get one. Fellowship with other people that believe because nobody is guaranteed tomorrow. What you decide to do with Jesus Christ and the gift of salvation He died for in order to make a way for us to be reconciled with God, is of eternal

---

[16] John 1:29
[17] Romans 6:23
[18] John 3:3
[19] 1 Peter 2:2,3

consequence. Your decision of whether to receive salvation in Christ and to follow Him, or to reject God's provision for the sin fallen human race, determines your eternal destiny. I am so thankful for the good news contained in the gospel of Jesus Christ, and that I can use my free will to decide to follow Jesus and have a relationship with God in this life and in the afterlife, when this short mortal venture is over upon my last breath and my spirit and soul leave my body to meet the Lord.

Enjoy life and walk at peace with God in your daily life, develop that relationship you have with God on this side of heaven throughout your mortal life and whether you will walk this earthly life in a vanquishing venture at peace with God as more than a conqueror, or by your choice you allow the devil to cause you to be a defeated foe through his tricks of lies and accusations and deceptions. Please don't allow yourself to be ripped off from the hope filled life and future God has for each of us. We can enact our free will to choose Jesus and enter a reconciled relationship with God.

Many people form their own opinions of what truth is, but we humans are like a speck of dust in the universe. How does all the knowledge we can gain in one short lifetime, and the opinions formed from that knowledge even be compared to God's omniscient wisdom and truth. Some seek wealth and have achieved much in one lifetime; but you can't take it with you. We are spiritual beings missing a relationship with God which created man originally had, and for which we truly deep-down thirst for whether an individual knows that or not; the pleasures of the world or wealth can only quench that thirst temporarily.

I implore you to humble yourself before our kind, loving and gracious heavenly Father. It's not a matter of saying, "I'm Catholic, I'm all set because I earned my salvation because of the sacraments."

No one can earn salvation, the bible stresses that salvation is a gift from God. It's not a matter of the good outweighing the bad like the scales of lady justice. If we could earn salvation, it would be like kicking Jesus in the teeth and saying there was no need for you to allow yourself to be brutalized and to sacrifice your life for me. Or some people might say, I'm protestant, and I was baptized, but they are far from following Jesus. Or some may say, but I am Jewish, don't you know I am one of God's chosen people? And yes, I do know that and respect that, but the word of God says, "For the life of the flesh is in the blood, and I have given it to you upon the altar to make atonement for your souls for it is the blood that makes atonement for the soul."[20] And I would encourage my Jewish friends to consider Jesus as the Lamb, the suffering servant of Isaiah 53, which gave His life for a new covenant in His blood brought into a heavenly temple not made with human hands.

The Jewish high priest used to sacrifice a lamb each year in the temple. I thank God that Jesus is the Messiah that did not come to set up an earthly kingdom like King Davids, which was expected; but through his death, burial and resurrection He has succeeded in taking away the sin of the world and has gone to prepare a kingdom, not of this world, whose mansions have many rooms. Upon the death of Jesus on the cross, "the veil of the temple was torn in two from top to bottom."[21] The old annual sacrifice gone, and a new covenant made through the sacrifice of the Lamb of God, once, for all time and for all humanity.

There are many other belief systems and religions trying to regain the broken relationship man had with God before the fall, but God only provided one way to be reconciled in relationship to Him, and

---

[20] Leviticus 17:11
[21] Matthew 27:51

that is through the good news of the finished work of Christ Jesus, the Messiah. The gospel is extended to whosoever would humble themselves before our awesome, kind and loving God to receive the gift of salvation by grace through faith. "For by grace you have been saved through faith, and that not of yourselves; it is the gift of God, not of works, lest anyone should boast."[22] Believe and repent! Have a change of heart and mind, and direction.

It is a matter of having childlike faith, and trust in our incredibly loving and kind God. God is so kind and longs to lead people to repentance. Don't complicate a reconciled relationship with God with mankind's traditions of religion, or rules or hoops you must jump through in order to be reconciled to God.

Have a heart-to-heart talk with God, reason together with God, acknowledge to Him that you are a sinner in need of a Savior and thank Him for His provision. "Come now, and let us reason together says the Lord, though your sins are like scarlet, they shall be as white as snow..."[23] Let God near to you as you humble yourself before His awesome presence. Get close to God.

There are several people that have had near death experiences to let us know that there is a heaven waiting, and others have let us know there is also an eternal place apart from God. This life is very short, and eternity is forever and yet people do not prepare for eternity by getting to know God, which is eternal life. "And this is eternal life, that they may know You, the only true God, and Jesus Christ whom You have sent."[24] People tend to prepare more for their short retirement years than for where they will spend all eternity. Our physical body will die someday, but that is just

---

[22] Ephesians 2:8,9
[23] Isaiah 1:18
[24] John 17 :3

our tent for the short mortal life we have here on earth. We are spiritual beings with a spirit and soul that will live for all eternity, and that eternal destination of being with God or apart from God, that choice is a huge decision, and millions have chosen the gift from God, but many others don't give eternity much consideration at all and will be lost forever, apart from God.

If I told people right now where they could go dig up a million dollars people would be in their cars starting them right now. I implore you to consider the seriousness of what I am trying to convey. I am encouraging people to develop a thirst for the bible. Discover with the help of Holy Spirit the gift of eternal life which is offered to you. "Seek the Lord while He may be found, call upon Him while He is near."[25]

Many households have Bibles, but people let them sit on the shelf collecting dust, which is very sad because that is spiritual food for you. Within the Bible are several books written by many authors over the course of approximately 1,500 years. Maybe start in one of the gospels of the New Testament, Matthew, Mark, Luke or John. Ask our Helper to help you understand the anointed, God breathed words of scripture. Men wrote the bible being inspired by the Holy Spirit of what exactly to write and the Holy Scriptures are God breathed.

The bible is like a GPS for our spiritual well-being. These days without a GPS system, many people would be totally lost out for a Sunday drive. I remember as a young man, trying to read a map and I said, "Wow, that's funny, that lake is supposed to be on the other side of the road." My friend said, "do you know what that means?" "We're going the wrong way." And, yes, we were going the

---

[25] Isaiah 55:6

wrong way. Many people are going the wrong way. "There is a way that seems right to a man, but its end is the way of death."[26] I am so grateful that God loves to find the lost and bring healing and soul restoration to us. He redirects us by His Spirit onto a new path.

Countries that know what real hunger is, they long for copies of the Bible. We are so spoiled here in America. I remember seeing a suitcase of Bibles that had been smuggled into a communist country which had an underground church because of persecution against Christians. When the person opened the suitcase, the people, in tears, lunged to get a copy. I heard that there were not enough bibles for everyone, so they would tear out the pages and memorize sections of the bible and pass the pages on to their neighbors. I pray; Renew our thirst Lord for your precious anointed word. We are so lost, we need you.

If Jesus remained dead in His tomb, Christianity would be futile. "And if Christ is not risen, your faith is futile; you are still in your sins."[27] It is such good news to know that Jesus won the victory over death. Three days after dying on the cross and being laid in a rich man's tomb, Jesus rose from the dead with resurrection power. I would say it is a good idea to get to know the One who overcame death, because we will all breathe our last breath one day and we will enter one of two destinations. Develop a holy reverent awe and respect for the Lord. "But I will show you whom you should fear. Fear Him who, after He has killed, has power to cast into hell; yes, I say to you, fear Him!"[28]

After Jesus rose from the dead over the next 40 days He appeared to many people. When He was nearing His time to ascend to heaven.

---

[26] Proverbs 14:12
[27] 1 Corinthians 15:17
[28] Luke 12:5

Jesus said that He would send us a Helper. I am so thankful for the Helper, God, the Holy Spirit. He encourages me, He helps me to understand the bible, opening my eyes reveling truth of the holy scriptures to me. God is the lifter of my head when I'm feeling down. He lets me know if I am going the wrong way so I can repent and ask God to forgive me and let Him cleanse me from the smear of sin. He gives me power to live at peace with myself, and with God. "If we confess our sins, He is faithful and just to forgive us our sins and to cleanse us from all unrighteousness."[29]

As we learn to abide in Jesus there is fruit of the Holy Spirit that starts to hang from the tree branches of our lives. We will start to have the fruit of His Holy Spirit evident in our lives: the fruit of love, joy, peace, patience, kindness, goodness, faithfulness, gentleness and self-control. So grateful to have this fruit rather than the rotten fruit which I used to have exemplifies my life. I am so grateful for the peace that God gives me as I keep my mind focused and re-focused on Him. I am grateful to be a blessed man because I trust in God, who is so worthy to be trusted, even though many in the past have misrepresented Him so much. I love the saying of one Christian brother that says, "I haven't arrived, but I left." Meaning there is always still more transformative work God will do in me this side of heaven, and I have not been perfected, but I left who I was. I need to be patient with myself in the process as I continue to put the roots of my life into the ways of the Lord.

In these days in which the principalities and powers of darkness are raising their ugly head, I highly encourage you and my friends and family to look to the ONE, and only hope God has provided for mankind. Please don't think of me as some type of religious nut. I have a reconciled relationship with God because of the Gospel of

---

[29] 1 John 1:9

Jesus Christ. God has been so merciful and kind to me. I encourage you to receive the help of Gods Holy Spirit to empower you to make a course correction which puts you on the narrow path which leads to life. Learn that what you are truly thirsty for in life is the living water which Jesus offers. All that the world has to offer may quench your thirst for a while, because there is pleasure in sin, but only for a season. Long for the living water Jesus offers, which alone can truly satisfy our thirst.

I have been clean and sober for over 22 years now, and I hope someone has been encouraged to get clean if you are using. I am not talking about a higher power here, I am talking about the power of the Most High, and He wants to empower us all to be free of any type of sin or bondage which has a foothold in our lives. And for those that don't deal with addiction, you need a Savior too because all of us have sinned, and I really pray you choose to allow yourself to be blessed with a reconciled relationship with God.

Thanks for reading, pass on the hope to others. Peace to you all!!!!

A few verses that mean a lot to consider and ponder:

"I waited patiently for the Lord; And He inclined to me. And heard my cry. He also brought me up out of a horrible pit. Out of the miry clay, and set my feet upon a rock, and established my steps. He has put a new song in my mouth- praise to God; Many will see it and fear and will trust in the Lord. Blessed is that man who makes the Lord his trust."[30]

"Let us therefore come boldly to the throne of grace, that we may obtain mercy and find grace to help in time of need."[31] (don't allow

---

[30] Psalm 40:1-4a

[31] Hebrews 4:16

the lies of satan to cause you to disqualify yourself from receiving the grace of God because of guilt, shame or self-condemnation.)

"...God resists the proud but gives grace to the humble. Therefore, submit to God. Resist the devil and he will flee from you. Draw near to God, and He will draw near to you...."[32]

"God has not given us a spirit of fear, but of power and of love and of a sound mind."[33]

"Jesus answered and said to him, "most assuredly, I say to you, unless one is born again, he cannot see the kingdom of God."[34]

"There is therefore now no condemnation to those who are in Christ Jesus who do not walk according to the flesh, but according to the Spirit."[35]

"Through the Lord's mercies we are not consumed, because His compassions fail not. They are new every morning; Great is Your faithfulness."[36]

"You will keep him in perfect peace, whose mind is stayed on You, because he trusts in You."[37]

"Jesus answered and said to her, "Whoever drinks of this water will thirst again, but whoever drinks of the water that I shall give him

---

[32] James 4:6b-8a
[33] 2 Timothy 1:7
[34] John 3:3
[35] Romans 8:1
[36] Lamentations 3:22,23
[37] Isaiah 26:3

will never thirst, but the water that I shall give him will become in him a fountain of water springing up into everlasting life."[38]

"Yet in all these things we are more than conquerors through Him who loved us. For I am persuaded that neither death nor life, nor angels nor principalities nor powers, nor things present nor things to come, nor height nor depth, nor any other created thing, shall be able to separate us from the love of God which is in Christ Jesus our Lord."[39]

To Christ Jesus be all glory, honor and praise. I will not let any lie, or accusation, or feelings of hopelessness or despair, nor guilt or shame, or any other tactic the enemy uses to make us condemn ourselves to make us disqualify ourselves from having a childlike, love relationship with God. We humble ourselves at the foot of the cross for the great exchange!

"Therefore, lay aside all filthiness and overflow of wickedness, and receive with meekness the implanted word, which is able to save your souls. But be doers of the word, and not hearers only, deceiving yourselves."[40]

"Do you not know that the unrighteous will not inherit the kingdom of God? DO NOT BE DECEIVED. Neither fornicators, nor idolaters, nor adulterers, nor homosexuals, nor sodomites, nor thieves, nor covetous, nor drunkards, nor revilers, nor extortioners will inherit the kingdom of God. And such WERE some of you. But you were washed, but you were sanctified, but you were justified in the name of the Lord Jesus and by the Spirit of our

---

[38] John 4:13,14
[39] Romans 8:37-39
[40] James 1:21,22

God."[41] I have not read too many times in the Bible where it says, "do not be deceived" We are living in a time where many have allowed themselves to be lied to and are deceived and deceptions are rampant in our modern society. God's truth brings freedom and is the remedy people are searching for, many just don't know it yet.

"Jesus said to her, "I am the resurrection and the life, He who believes in Me, though he may die, he shall live. And whoever lives and believes in Me shall never die. Do you believe this?"[42]

"Now thanks be to God who always leads us in triumph in Christ, and through us diffuses the fragrance of His knowledge in every place."[43]

The Lord God almighty is longing to hear from YOU!!!! He is so worthy of our trust. Blessings and Peace to you!!!

---

[41] 1 Corinthians 6:9-11
[42] John 11:25,26
[43] 2 Corinthians 2:14